ULTRA Cheer

A CHRISTMAS KEEPSAKE SCRAPBOOK

Amaranthine Arts

How To Use

Gather 'Round! Use this workbook as a shared family activity throughout Christmas Day—whether it's morning, around the tree, or after the feast.

Reflect & Share! Each page invites reflection on gratitude, memories, and moments from this Christmas celebration. Encourage everyone to join in!

Create Traditions! Begin new family customs with activities like Recipe Share and Christmas Memories pages.

Interactive Fun! Enjoy word searches, mazes, and other games to add dash of holiday cheer to your day.

Capture the Spirit! Use prompts to record the atmosphere, memorable moments, and heartfelt conversations this Christmas.

Involve Everyone! Activities are designed for all ages—kids can draw and play while adults reflect.

Make It Yours! Add photos, notes, stickers, and drawings to create a unique family Christmas keepsake.

End on Cheer! Enjoy the final affirmation pages, share thoughts and look ahead to the cheers of the coming year.

This Christmas

Unwrap the joy, capture the magic, and celebrate those who make your hearts merry this season!

♥ LisaMaria

What's The Year?

have yourself
A MERRY
LITTLE
Christmas

Who's Here?

BE · OUR
GUEST

What's On The Menu?

Best Dish Of The Day

yum

Share A RECIPE

What's The Vibe?

Soundtrack Of The Day

Season's Best Laughs

HA
HA HA

ho-ho-ho

Christmas Toast

Holiday Cheers!

Make A Christmas Wish!

What Are You Looking Forward To?

Favorite Holiday Scents

Warmest Winter Memory

Favorite Christmas Activity

Best Gifts

XOXO

Holiday Heartfelt Moments

Moments of *kindness*

Draw Or Paste A Family Photo

What Fills Your Heart With Cheer?

Christmas Signature Pages

Merry Christmas
BEST WISHES
And A Very
Happy
New Year

Spot The Differences

Christmas Word Search

I	Q	J	P	Q	L	E	W	C	I	O	J	B	J	L	I	W	A	I	X
T	T	H	A	P	P	Y	T	G	V	T	L	J	O	X	Q	Q	T	Z	G
B	O	Q	H	O	L	I	D	A	Y	S	R	I	L	N	U	B	F	K	S
L	G	S	G	O	S	I	W	U	M	E	V	E	L	W	G	Z	S	G	Q
O	E	C	Z	R	O	O	J	H	E	X	Y	D	Y	S	V	A	N	Q	G
B	T	C	P	C	R	K	Z	T	R	J	K	D	T	D	M	I	D	M	N
O	H	E	N	H	N	K	Y	G	R	L	I	N	N	T	T	T	R	E	E
G	E	L	G	I	A	O	V	G	Y	Y	E	F	S	E	L	Z	Y	T	J
C	R	S	P	M	M	B	W	P	H	S	Z	I	E	B	J	E	R	A	A
M	N	L	B	N	E	E	N	O	E	H	R	R	O	W	I	R	G	C	S
N	E	E	G	E	N	Z	H	R	J	H	G	G	E	D	C	D	P	O	S
W	S	I	V	Y	T	N	P	A	C	H	L	T	C	H	E	E	R	S	R
J	S	G	X	L	S	X	A	P	K	I	N	D	N	E	S	S	L	J	M
P	C	H	T	D	U	Q	T	N	D	L	S	E	U	U	B	E	V	B	R
W	B	N	P	Z	Q	X	E	U	Q	A	C	B	R	V	G	U	I	O	J
H	G	O	O	I	E	X	C	L	B	P	G	E	D	N	K	W	I	R	L
J	B	P	T	R	A	D	I	T	I	O	N	L	A	L	C	Q	O	K	G
L	B	W	O	N	D	E	R	L	A	N	D	L	C	T	N	Q	X	P	H
M	C	X	J	C	F	L	Y	I	Q	W	Q	S	O	K	B	M	C	F	L
G	C	G	A	M	J	F	Q	P	J	U	I	F	A	M	I	L	Y	E	H

ANGELS BELLS CHRISTMAS CHEER CHIMNEY EVE

FAMILY GREETINGS HAPPY HOLIDAYS JOLLY KINDNESS

MERRY ORNAMENTS PRESENTS SLEIGH TRADITION TREE

TOGETHERNESS WONDERLAND

Unscramble The Words

OETMLSEIT ____________________

CMREEEDB ____________________

RNWIET ____________________

STHILG ____________________

RCSALO ____________________

PFIARCELE ____________________

EDRIAGBNREG ____________________

LYHLO ____________________

TKOINSGC ____________________

NEIERDRE ____________________

YRERM ____________________

STMHIARSC ____________________

YFTROS ____________________

ECELUHFR ____________________

My heart is open to joy
and connection this
Christmas.

My life is rich with love
and laughter this season.

I give and receive with an
open heart.

I cherish the little moments that make this season special.

I am grateful for the love
and joy around me.

I create beautiful memories
with the people I love.

I am present, grateful, and
joyful today.

Each day, I welcome
happiness and love.

I savor the simple joys of
the season.

I share my light and lift
others around me.

The season brings me
inspiration and hope.

I create warmth and
connection in my home.

I choose to focus on joy
and gratitude.

I hold space for laughter
and meaningful moments.

I celebrate the love that
brings us together.

I carry the spirit of giving
in my heart.

I feel warmth and love
surrounding me.

I find joy in every cozy,
winter moment.

I treasure the connections
that the season brings.

I feel deeply grateful for
the blessings in my life.

I celebrate the gift of time
with loved ones.

I let go of expectations
and enjoy the present.

I embrace the magic of
giving with an open heart.

I welcome each holiday
moment with gratitude.

I choose to see the
goodness in each day.

I celebrate the little
wonders all around me.

I hold space for calm
amidst the holiday hustle.

I am mindful of the joy
and love around me.

I am grateful for the quiet moments of reflection.

I breathe in peace and
breathe out gratitude.

I cherish each moment as
it unfolds, without hurry.

SOLUTIONS

SOLUTIONS

I	Q	J	P	Q	L	E	W	C	I	O	J	B	J	L	I	W	A	I	X
T	T	H	A	P	P	Y	T	G	V	T	L	J	O	X	Q	Q	T	Z	G
B	O	Q	H	O	L	I	D	A	Y	S	R	I	L	N	U	B	F	K	S
L	G	S	G	O	S	I	W	U	M	E	V	E	L	W	G	Z	S	G	Q
O	E	C	Z	R	O	O	J	H	E	X	Y	D	Y	S	V	A	N	Q	G
B	T	C	P	C	R	K	Z	T	R	J	K	D	T	D	M	I	D	M	N
O	H	E	N	H	N	K	Y	G	R	L	I	N	N	T	T	T	R	E	E
G	E	L	G	I	A	O	V	G	Y	Y	E	F	S	E	L	Z	Y	T	J
C	R	S	P	M	M	B	W	P	H	S	Z	I	E	B	J	E	R	A	A
M	N	L	B	N	E	E	N	O	E	H	R	R	O	W	I	R	G	C	S
N	E	E	G	E	N	Z	H	R	J	H	G	G	E	D	C	D	P	O	S
W	S	I	V	Y	T	N	P	A	C	H	L	T	C	H	E	E	R	S	R
J	S	G	X	L	S	X	A	P	K	I	N	D	N	E	S	S	L	J	M
P	C	H	T	D	U	Q	T	N	D	L	S	E	U	U	B	E	V	B	R
W	B	N	P	Z	Q	X	E	U	Q	A	C	B	R	V	G	U	I	O	J
H	G	O	O	I	E	X	C	L	B	P	G	E	D	N	K	W	I	R	L
J	B	P	T	R	A	D	I	T	I	O	N	L	A	L	C	Q	O	K	G
L	B	W	O	N	D	E	R	L	A	N	D	L	C	T	N	Q	X	P	H
M	C	X	J	C	F	L	Y	I	Q	W	Q	S	O	K	B	M	C	F	L
G	C	G	A	M	J	F	Q	P	J	U	I	F	A	M	I	L	Y	E	H

ANGELS BELLS CHRISTMAS CHEER CHIMNEY EVE
FAMILY GREETINGS HAPPY HOLIDAYS JOLLY KINDNESS
MERRY ORNAMENTS PRESENTS SLEIGH TRADITION TREE
TOGETHERNESS WONDERLAND

SOLUTIONS

OETMLSEIT	MISTLETOE
CMREEEDB	DECEMBER
RNWIET	WINTER
STHILG	LIGHTS
RCSALO	CAROLS
PFIARCELE	FIREPLACE
EDRIAGBNREG	GINGERBREAD
LYHLO	HOLLY
TKOINSGC	STOCKING
NEIERDRE	REINDEER
YRERM	MERRY
STMHIARSC	CHRISTMAS
YFTROS	FROSTY
ECELUHFR	CHEERFUL

SOLUTIONS

It's the most Wonderful time of the year

Merry Christmas!

A Little About Me

ARTIST
ILLUSTRATOR
SOFTWARE ENGINEER
GRAPHIC DESIGNER
CALLIGRAPHER
WRITER

amaranthinearts.com
hello@amaranthinearts.com

Made in the USA
Columbia, SC
02 November 2024

45496528R00042